Waiting in Joyful Hope

*Daily Reflections for
Advent and Christmas
2017–2018*

Mary DeTurris Poust

LITURGICAL PRESS

Collegeville, Minnesota

www.litpress.org

Nihil Obstat: Reverend Robert Harren, J.C.L., *Censor deputatus.*
Imprimatur: ✠ Most Reverend Donald J. Kettler, J.C.L., Bishop of Saint Cloud, Minnesota. March 16, 2017.

Cover design by Monica Bokinskie. Cover photo © Thinkstock.

ISSN: 1550-803X
ISBN: 978-0-8146-4689-2   978-0-8146-4734-9 (ebook)

Introduction

I'll admit right up front that for most of my life I considered myself a Lent person more than an Advent person. I was more comfortable in the desert than in the midst of party preparations. But slowly, slowly, as I aged, I began to "get" Advent, which really is a desert experience of a very different kind. Unlike Lent, where the desert is obvious and clear, Advent beckons us to seek out a hidden desert, our interior desert, the dry places in our spiritual lives that need to be worked out and made lush before the coming of Jesus Christ—both in celebration on Christmas Day and again at the end of all time.

As we begin our journey toward Christmas, we have to be careful not to pay too much attention to the flashy decorations and nostalgic carols that threaten to rob us of this waiting time and rush us into a moment that is not yet here. We do that through the rhythm of Advent, a season that challenges us to slow down even as the drumbeat of commercial Christmas pounds out its "Hurry! Hurry!" warning. This is a time of silence and darkness, waiting and watching, surrender and trust.

The flickering candles of the Advent wreath burn through the enveloping blackness of early December evenings to remind us week by week that the dark will never overcome us. Light is coming—on Christmas and for all time—but we must be patient. This is the season of waiting, a long pregnant pause, full of expectant joy, much like a mother waiting for labor to begin, much like Mary waiting for the arrival of her Son. We, too, wait, perhaps not so patiently but through prayer and silence, growing more ripe each day, more ready for what is to come, *who* is to come.

As we walk this path through Advent, into Christmas, and right out the other side back toward Ordinary Time, we do not travel alone. We walk with fellow travelers who surround us, sometimes physically when we gather at church or around the dinner table for a meal, sometimes virtually as we talk and pray together through social media or email or texting, and sometimes invisibly from the other side, the communion of saints that carries us along in and out of season through prayer and intercession.

In the crisp, cold air of winter we will feel a warm glow burning stronger and stronger inside, filling our desert spaces with light and life, until our hearts cry out, *Maranatha*, "O Lord, come!" And then there will be celebration for the One who comes into the world to save it, the incarnation that makes us gasp in wonder and bow in humility. Jesus Christ is born, giving us reason to sing with joy to the world, a feast that doesn't last a day but has a season all to itself, taking us through the octave of Christmas, the feast of the Holy Family, the solemnity of Mary, saints' feast days, the Epiphany, and, finally, the Baptism of our Lord.

What a whirlwind of spiritual anticipation and celebration is in store for us! Let us begin, slowly, silently at first, until we can contain ourselves no longer. O come, O come, Emmanuel . . .

FIRST WEEK OF ADVENT

Keeping God at Arm's Length

Readings: Isa 63:16b-17, 19b; 64:2-7; 1 Cor 1:3-9; Mark 13:33-37

Scripture:
Why do you let us wander, O LORD, from your ways,
  and harden our hearts so that we fear you not?
    (Isa 63:17)

Reflection: It's funny how we humans can find ways to blame God for everything, even our own indifference. "Why do you let us wander, O Lord, from your ways . . ." we hear in today's first reading. Even when we harden our hearts and distance ourselves from God, we act as though God should be chasing us down, making us stay, like petulant children who need to be forced to obey our parents. But that is not how God's love works. God also gives us free will and allows us to make our own choices, even if the choice is to keep him at arm's length.

Today, as we begin our Advent journey, we have a chance to start over, to reflect on the ways we have pushed God away. "Be watchful! Be alert!" the Gospel of Mark reminds us, making clear that we need to get our spiritual house in order. Now is the time. This is our season. God has not abandoned us in the desert or left us to wander without a guide. He waits, patiently, for us to choose him willingly, for us to recognize that when we find ourselves lost and faltering it is because we have abandoned God, not the other way around. On this first day of Advent, we have a choice, as we do every day, every moment. Do we plan to go it alone, or will we anchor ourselves to the One who will never leave us?

Meditation: Stop everything you are doing and think about the last few months of your life. Were there times when you felt the way the people of Israel did in the reading from Isaiah? Have you felt abandoned by God, adrift in the chaos of life? Now reflect on your spiritual journey. Did the times you felt alone coincide with the times you didn't make time for prayer, didn't make time for God? Today, as we take the first step on our path through Advent, let us recommit ourselves to being alert to the Lord moving through our days, even when we are going in the wrong direction.

Prayer: Dear Lord, we know that we are not always attentive to you or grateful for the ways you give meaning to our days. Help us to remember that you will never leave us to wander this life lost and alone. You are there. Always.

December 4: Monday of the First Week of Advent

Healing Graces

Readings: Isa 2:1-5; Matt 8:5-11

Scripture:
The centurion said in reply,
>"Lord, I am not worthy to have you enter under my
>   roof;
>only say the word and my servant will be healed."
>   (Matt 8:8)

Reflection: A few years back, when the church instituted changes to the Roman Missal, I struggled with some of the new language of the Mass. I was of the if-it-ain't-broke-don't-fix-it mindset. But then something happened. As I said the new version of the prayer just before Communion, I had an epiphany of sorts. "Lord, I am not worthy / that you should enter under my roof, . . . " and suddenly I had a vision of the centurion, a nonbeliever who had more belief than I do, it seems. The words of that Scripture verse, the same ones we hear in today's gospel, are among my favorites. Each time I say that phrase, I am reminded of the kind of faith I am supposed to have, faith enough to believe without question that just a word from Jesus can heal me, or you, or anyone.

But we are given much more than a word. We are given bread from heaven, Jesus himself. Even as we prepare to celebrate the birth of Jesus, we are reminded again and again that it was through the death of Jesus that we are saved. A faith of paradoxes, a gift beyond reason. And we, like the centurion, are reminded that if we go to Jesus in faith, no matter what else might be going on in our lives, he will give us his healing grace, maybe not in the exact way we expect or want but in a way that will no doubt transform us as it did the servant and the centurion long ago.

Meditation: Put yourself in the crowd with Jesus as the centurion comes to him asking for healing for his servant. Imagine the shock that rippled through the crowd as this Roman—the enemy—sought a gift that others probably felt should be reserved only for those of outward and obvious faith. Jesus shows us otherwise. Faith does not always look the way we expect it to look, but it has power just the same. What do you need Jesus to heal in your life today?

Prayer: Jesus, how we wish we could speak to you, touch the hem of your garment, know what it means to be in your presence. Today we pray for the faith of the centurion, who believed without needing anything more than a word from you. Heal our hearts and increase our faith.

December 5: Tuesday of the First Week of Advent

Creating a Sea Change

Readings: Isa 11:1-10; Luke 10:21-24

Scripture:
There shall be no harm or ruin on all my holy mountain;
   for the earth shall be filled with knowledge of the LORD,
   as water covers the sea. (Isa 11:9)

Reflection: If you've ever had a chance to stare out at the ocean, you know there is a vastness there that almost defies human comprehension. That's why I love the beach so much. As I stand there on the shore, looking out at endless water meeting endless sky, I recognize my own smallness and God's greatness. I think that's why I was so struck by this line from today's first reading from Isaiah: "for the earth shall be filled with knowledge of the LORD, / as water covers the sea." What was that supposed to mean then? What does it mean now?

I try to imagine a world where knowledge of the Lord has the same vastness as my beloved ocean, and I realize what a wonderful—and vastly different—world we would be living in if that were the case. Trapped as we are in our own human ideas about God and our conflicting religious and political and ideological beliefs, we are instead flooded with tension and anger and misunderstanding rather than love and mercy and solidarity. And it's easy to feel hopeless. How can we bring about this sea change, so to speak, when the world's problems seem so big?

Saint Teresa of Calcutta left us with this reminder: "I want you to find the poor here, right in your own home first. And begin love there. Be that good news to your own people."

Meditation: When you look at the daily headlines or scroll through your social media feeds, do you ever get a feeling that there's just no use? What's the point of getting involved and being engaged if we can't effect change? But that kind of apathy doesn't spread the Gospel, not in the world, not in our own communities, not in our own families. We need to begin at home, maybe even within. Before we start with our family, we must start with ourselves. As the classic song says, "Let there be peace on earth, and let it begin with me."

Prayer: Creator God, we look out at the world around us and see the vastness of your love. Give us the courage to share that love through the example of our lives so that we may bring about a change for the good one person at a time.

Food for the Journey

Readings: Isa 25:6-10a; Matt 15:29-37

Scripture:
"I do not want to send them away hungry,
    for fear they may collapse on the way." (Matt 15:32)

Reflection: At times in my past, I have used the Eucharist as a weapon—against myself. Although it wouldn't happen frequently, there would be times when I'd skip Communion out of some sort of internal protest. Perhaps I yelled at one of my children or had an argument with my husband on the way to Mass. Maybe I was angry with God over some life obstacle that had left me frustrated. I'd stay in my pew feeling one of two ways: sad that I was such a failure as a Christian or, conversely, mad and on some level convinced that skipping Communion was a way to stick it to God. I know, it's amazing I haven't been struck by lightning.

In today's gospel reading, Jesus says something that applies not only to the hungry crowd milling about the hillside but to those of us mucking around in our own self-made crises. Jesus knows we are weary. He knows we are sad or mad or tired or losing hope, and he does not want us to go away hungry. I finally learned that, due in part to a pastor who continually reminded our congregation that Communion was for the weak, not the strong.

I'm still far from worthy to receive Jesus on any given Sunday, no matter how prepared I might be, but these days I won't skip Eucharist for no good reason because I know that without it there's a very good chance I might collapse—at least spiritually—on my way through the world. Jesus gives us himself in abundance because he knows we need sustenance. Don't pass up the food he offers.

Meditation: Today's familiar story of Jesus feeding the multitudes is easy to overlook. We've heard it so many times, we think we know it. Read it again. Slowly. How does it speak to you? Are you among the hungry throng? Are you one of the disciples wanting to send the crowd away rather than figure out a way to feed them? What do Jesus' words mean to you? Will you let him feed you so you don't collapse?

Prayer: Thank you, dear Jesus, for recognizing that we need food for the journey. Although we might not ever be worthy of the gift of Eucharist, we ask you to forgive us and accept us so that we may receive you and be strengthened for whatever lies ahead.

December 7: Saint Ambrose, Bishop and Doctor
of the Church

God Is My Fortress

Readings: Isa 26:1-6; Matt 7:21, 24-27

Scripture:
Trust in the LORD forever!
    For the LORD is an eternal Rock. (Isa 26:4)

Reflection: We get quite a visual juxtaposition in today's readings, from God the eternal Rock in Isaiah to the fool who built his house on sand in Matthew's gospel. Where do we fit in? Have we chosen one or the other, or are we stranded somewhere unsure, somewhere in between? These two images hit home for me since I live between the magnificent Adirondack and Catskill Mountains but spend at least a little time each summer on the sandy shores of the New Jersey coast. I am always amazed by the fact that within the span of just a few hours I can have both, the towering strength of rock and the soft pliancy of sand.

Of course, as the mother of three, I've watched my children build their share of sandcastles on those beaches. They'd carefully craft turrets and bridges decorated with shells and stones and then tearfully watch it all vanish bit by bit, or sometimes all at once, as the tide came in and knocked out its foundation or overwhelmed its walls. Today's gospel reminds us that if we are not careful about where we build our lives, we, too, could be swept out into a sea of materialism, power, envy, greed, despair that threatens to overwhelm us or even drown us.

"Everyone who listens to these words of mine and acts on them / will be like a wise man who built his house on rock," Jesus says. Today we hear his words, but do we act on them? Where have we chosen to build our house?

Meditation: Scripture often uses the beauty and power of our natural world to remind us of our place in God's plan, and today is no exception. What image comes to mind when you see God as an "eternal Rock"? Can you stake your life there? What do you need to do to shore up the moorings of your own "house" so that it can withstand life's battering storms—death and job loss, marriage and parenting problems, illness and financial strife? Without a rock to anchor you, the undertow will set you adrift.

Prayer: Heavenly Father, give us the courage and grace to turn away from the easy path, the world's ways, and build our future on the strength of your promises, your unchanging love and mercy.

December 8:
Immaculate Conception of the Blessed Virgin Mary
(Catholic Church)

Friday of the First Week of Advent
(Episcopal Church)

To Jesus through Mary

Readings: Gen 3:9-15, 20; Eph 1:3-6, 11-12; Luke 1:26-38

Scripture:
And coming to her, he said,
"Hail, full of grace! The Lord is with you." (Luke 1:28)

Reflection: Today's feast day focuses on how Mary is different from us, immaculately conceived, something that's hard for us to wrap our human minds around. We tend to put all of our focus on how Jesus was conceived, and the fact that today's gospel focuses on the annunciation doesn't help matters. But this day is about what sets our Blessed Mother apart. She was highly "favored" by God, set apart, the new Eve, and through her fiat, her "yes" to God's will, she begins the course correction for our first parents' mistakes.

The only danger, however, is that this special status tends to keep Mary up on a pedestal, bound to the title Queen of Heaven, when what makes her so important and special is the way she acted in the ordinariness of her extraordinary life. She was a young girl given a monumental responsibility that she didn't fully understand. She was a mother whose life was fraught with the worries and fears of any other mother—about her child's well-being and safety, caring for her home, practicing her faith. Her life had to be difficult and scary, confusing and demanding, which many of us experience in our own day-to-day lives.

That's what makes Mary so special. We can go to her and to her Son through her because she has been where we are. She has seen it all, despite the extraordinary way her life began. She will walk with us and be a mother to us just as she was a mother to Jesus. As we read on the miraculous medal and pray now, "O Mary, conceived without sin, pray for us who have recourse to thee."

Meditation: For many of us the Hail Mary is the first prayer we learn as children. What does that prayer mean to you now? Hear it as if for the first time today, and imagine Mary listening to you as your earthly mother might. What does she say to you? What does she offer you? Comfort? Consolation? Peace? Jesus gave you his mother as your own. Take him at his word and trust her to lead you closer to him.

Prayer: Mary, Mother of God, we turn to you in gratitude for your "yes" to God and for your "yes" to us today. Lead us closer to your Son so that we might one day know the fullness of heaven in the company of all the angels and saints.

The Smell of the Sheep

Readings: Isa 30:19-21, 23-26; Matt 9:35–10:1, 5a, 6-8

Scripture:
At the sight of the crowds, his heart was moved with pity
    for them
  because they were troubled and abandoned,
  like sheep without a shepherd. (Matt 9:36)

Reflection: Soon after Pope Francis was elected, he implored his bishops and priests to "be shepherds, with the 'odour of the sheep.'" He sensed that people were hungry, desperate for shepherds who would not just tell them about God from the pulpit on Sunday but who would show them about God in the sometimes sorrowful, sometimes joyful moments of everyday life. I remember tears coming to my eyes when I read the pope's words because at that point in my life my heart and spirit were crying out for that same kind of shepherd.

Jesus seems moved, in today's gospel, for those very same reasons. He looks around and sees a people who appear to be troubled and abandoned, like sheep without a shepherd, and so he tells his disciples to go out to the "lost sheep," to cure the sick and drive out demons.

I think if Jesus were on a crowded plaza in our world today, he'd likely think the same thing. People are troubled and abandoned, evident in the rise in depression, drug and alcohol use, suicide, pornography, and more. As a society, we are not doing a very good job of shepherding ourselves. We need to seek out those who can shepherd us, whether that's our pastor, our spouse, our parent, a friend with whom we share a close spiritual bond, or perhaps a confessor we may not know at all.

Meditation: Most of us have so much on our plate these days that "troubled" seems like it comes with this territory called life. And yet, when we begin to dwell in that place full-time, we become cynical and selfish. We need a shepherd to call us back home and remind us we are loved. Jesus is that eternal shepherd, the One who is always available to us, but it's good to have someone in our life who can check in with us and help us stay on track day after day. Do you have someone in your life who serves as a spiritual shepherd? Call or write to that person today.

Prayer: Jesus you are the Good Shepherd, the one who leads us home whenever we are lost. Today we pray for the understanding and vision to know and see when we are veering off course and to get the help we need to strengthen our resolve and our faith.

SECOND WEEK OF ADVENT

December 10: Second Sunday of Advent

What Time Is It?

Readings: Isa 40:1-5, 9-11; 2 Pet 3:8-14; Mark 1:1-8

Scripture:
Do not ignore this one fact, beloved,
   that with the Lord one day is like a thousand years
   and a thousand years like one day. (2 Pet 3:8)

Reflection: I think many of us see time as the enemy. There are simply not enough hours in the day. If only I had an extra hour, an extra day, an extra week. Or, during times of suffering when we lie awake at night or times of waiting when we anticipate a visit, a call, a letter, time seems to stand still. I wish it were tomorrow, next week, next year.

In today's Second Letter of Peter, we are reminded that our focus on time and its passing is very different from the Lord's version of time, which is endless and finite all at once. We simply cannot grasp a concept of time that works like that, not according to clocks, not bound by empty boxes on a wall calendar.

We are told that God is patient, not wishing for us to perish, and at the same time that God will come "like a thief in the night" and dissolve the heavens in flames. This is another paradox, another deep lesson calling us to look at the way we live our lives and the way we see time. Often we think we have plenty of it. There's always tomorrow, we tell ourselves.

Right now, my family is praying daily for three people battling cancer: a child, a mother of four, and a priest. None of these people could have imagined time would play out for them in this way, and yet here they are. The mom with cancer, a dear friend, says she wants to live her life for as long as she can in as normal a way as she can for her family. She understands time. She may not have much of it, and so she should live like she is dying. The same goes for the rest of us.

Meditation: How often do you tackle a chore all the while wishing it was over so you could get onto the next thing? It's a struggle to live in the present. Today's readings remind us that we need to make straight our ways today. God doesn't operate from a day planner, and, when it comes to the big stuff in life, neither should we. Be. Here. Now.

Prayer: God of the universe, your promise of eternity is a gift beyond comprehension. Help us to appreciate the moments that make up daily life and spend our time in ways that celebrate our blessings.

Incredible Things

Readings: Isa 35:1-10; Luke 5:17-26

Scripture:
Then astonishment seized them all and they glorified God,
    and, struck with awe, they said,
    "We have seen incredible things today." (Luke 5:26)

Reflection: Over and over, throughout my life, the Lord has done incredible things. Sometimes those things were magnificently wonderful, like the birth of my three children. Sometimes those things were heartbreakingly awful, like the death of my mother and the miscarriage of my second baby. And sometimes those things were ordinarily simple, like the letters received at exactly the right moment, the billboard message when I needed to read it, the beautiful broken shell washed ashore at my feet.

With every incredible thing, I can remember thinking *this* is it; I will never be the same. So convinced was I of God's presence in my life—palpable, touchable, visible—that I knew in my heart I had reached the moment I had been waiting for: complete inner transformation. And it would make a difference for at least a few days or, in the case of deep pain and joy, a few precious months. But little by little the wonder lost its awe—not really but in my mind. I began to forget what I had seen and slip back into my cynical ways and complaints about not feeling God's presence in my life.

I wonder if that's what it was like for some of the people in today's gospel. They saw incredible things and glorified God. For how long? I wonder if any of them were in the crowd saying, "Crucify him." Would I be in the crowd? Or would the incredible works of Jesus, seen up close, have changed my heart and mind forever?

Meditation: As we move through Advent and closer to Christmas, we are well aware that something incredible awaits us. During this season of darkness and light, we know that hope is our birthright thanks to the birth, death, and resurrection of Jesus Christ. Do you lose sight of that gift during Ordinary Time? Can you hold onto your Advent awe when Christmas has come and gone?

Prayer: Incarnate God, we wait in awe for your arrival in a manger and your second coming at the end of the world. Renew our hearts and give us the grace to glorify your name always, to continue to bear witness to the incredible things you continue to do in our lives and our world every day.

December 12:
Our Lady of Guadalupe
(Catholic Church)

Tuesday of the Second Week of Advent
(Episcopal Church)

Unwrapping the "Real" Mary

Readings: Zech 2:14-17 or Rev 11:19a; 12:1-6a, 10ab; Luke 1:26-38 or Luke 1:39-47

Scripture:
Silence, all mankind, in the presence of the LORD!
  For he stirs forth from his holy dwelling. (Zech 2:17)

Reflection: Our Lady of Guadalupe has a special place in my heart. If you knew my backstory, you might think that's due to the fact that I've lived in Texas twice in my life, and Our Lady of Guadalupe looms large in the Lone Star State, both as a spiritual role model and a cultural icon. But I came by way of Our Lady of Guadalupe through my Irish Catholic grandfather as he lay dying. A pilgrim image of the tilma of Juan Diego was hung in the downstairs room of his house that had become a makeshift hospital room.

My grandfather was a man of faith, deep faith, deeper than any faith I have ever known, and our Blessed Mother was pivotal in his prayer life, so it made sense to hang an image of Mary near him as he neared the end. And yet Our Lady of Guadalupe was an unusual choice for him. I was intrigued by her then and eventually fell in love with her because she was so real. She was not a queen on a pedestal wearing a crown of gold but a peasant who looked like the people she came to comfort. Suddenly I could relate to my namesake, who had often seemed so distant.

If you look around my house and my office, Our Lady of Guadalupe is everywhere—in my garden, in my kitchen, in my family room, over a conference table, behind my desk. Seeing her image immediately brings me comfort and reminds me that miracles happen and I have a spiritual mother who will help them along their way, even when I don't recognize them for the miracles they are.

Meditation: Reflect on your image of Mary. Is she far away, a queen beyond reach, or is she a mother struggling to raise a Son and understanding all of the pains and joys of human life? Try to strip away the artistic interpretations that may obscure the real Blessed Mother from view. She is there for you, every day, with comfort and concern and arms outstretched, ready to take your prayers to her Son.

Prayer: Hail Mary, full of grace, wrap us in your mantel, shelter us in your arms as we journey toward heaven. Hear our prayers and carry them to the heart of your Son. To Jesus through Mary.

December 13:
Saint Lucy, Virgin and Martyr
(Catholic Church)

Wednesday of the Second Week of Advent
(Episcopal Church)

Spiritual Rubbernecking

Readings: Isa 40:25-31; Matt 11:28-30

Scripture:
They that hope in the LORD will renew their strength,
    they will soar as with eagles' wings;
They will run and not grow weary,
    walk and not grow faint. (Isa 40:31)

Reflection: Not long ago, a woman I'd known only through some work-related social media attended a spiritual talk I was giving. We connected immediately, realizing we had already connected virtually, and we set a date to chat privately. As I was bemoaning some issues surrounding a project I was working on, she said wisely, just as she was about to leave, "This is just the machinery; don't confuse it with the way."

I'm not sure she realized what a profound statement she was making at that time or how powerful it would be in the days and weeks ahead, but it's become a silent mantra of mine, reminding me that there will be lots of frustrating and sometimes humiliating obstacles along the path to heaven, and we're only in danger when we take our eyes off the road to look at the accidents on the shoulder. It's sort of a spiritual version of highway rubbernecking, and just as dangerous.

Today's reading from Isaiah brought my friend's comment back to the forefront of my mind. As I read the prophet's reminder that God will keep us strong when we are failing and give us wings to soar like an eagle, I saw my path suddenly clear for the first time in a long time. Other people may push obstacles in our way; God gives us the courage and the grace to sidestep them or leap over them. Go ahead, jump.

Meditation: What obstacles have kept you from progressing on the Way? Is there something in your life right now that's sapping your energy and distracting you from God's voice whispering in your ear? Shut it all out for a few minutes. Turn off your phone and computer. Turn off the TV or radio. Just sit and listen, for five minutes, or twenty if you dare. Let the thoughts come and go without a fight. Do that every day and your life will be transformed from the inside out.

Prayer: Holy Spirit, we know you are trying to speak to us amid the chaos of our lives. Teach us to listen with the ear of our heart and to make space for sacred silence apart from the world around us.

December 14:
Saint John of the Cross
(Catholic Church)

Thursday of the Second Week of Advent
(Episcopal Church)

Plugging Our Ears

Readings: Isa 41:13-20; Matt 11:11-15

Scripture:
"Whoever has ears ought to hear." (Matt 11:15)

Reflection: My younger daughter, Chiara, doesn't like to play board games that require timers. The tick, tick, ticking in her ear as she's trying to come up with answers quickly distracts her and she can't think clearly. What she's hearing is getting in the way of what she's thinking. I can understand where she's coming from. If you've ever turned down the car radio when you're looking for a street in an unfamiliar neighborhood, you get the idea. Our hearing, our seeing, and our thinking are all interconnected.

Today Jesus speaks of John the Baptist in ways that were probably confusing to the people of his time and confusing to us today, and he ends by saying, "Whoever has ears ought to hear." The funny thing is, when I read that line I immediately think of Chiara putting her fingers in her ears as she tries to come up with three quick answers in under five seconds. I feel like I need to put my fingers in my ears in order to hear Jesus clearly, to get the full meaning of what he's saying.

We often think our lives today are busier and more difficult than the lives of those who've come before us, but the truth is that people have always had busy and difficult lives, often far more difficult than what any of us have to deal with. And, like us, I'm sure they became distracted by the "noise" of their day, the intermingling voices that carried the news and the gossip and the truth. Jesus, as always, recognizes the human tendency to listen to the wrong thing and tries to remind them and us that we need to block out the tick, tick, ticking of the world.

Meditation: Stop what you're doing and listen. What do you hear? If your house is like mine, you can probably hear the heat running, the phone ringing, the washing machine spinning, the faucet dripping. Sounds can get in the way of our hearing and keep us from focusing on the important messages. What are you paying attention to today? What's playing in the background that might be calling out to you?

Prayer: God of wisdom, you know our hearts. Help us to hear your voice among the many. Let us hear your message and understand its meaning in our lives. Give us ears to hear.

December 15: Friday of the Second Week of Advent

Working Up to Wisdom

Readings: Isa 48:17-19; Matt 11:16-19

Scripture:
" . . . wisdom is vindicated by her works." (Matt 11:19b)

Reflection: We humans have a lot to prove, at least that's how we tend to live our lives—trying to prove our worth by the amount of money we have, the title that hangs on our office door, the neighborhood where we live. A few days spent on social media makes it painfully obvious that we are all wearing masks—maybe not all the time but often, in order to be what we think people want us to be, to be lovable, to be successful, maybe even to be envied.

Jesus will have none of that. In today's gospel, he reminds us that life is often a no-win situation from the world's point of view. The people didn't like John the Baptist's fasting and they didn't like the Son of Man's feasting. Nothing would please them, because it wasn't really about John or Jesus; it was about them and their need to feel superior, righteous, in control.

How often do we look at others and tsk-tsk over something of which we do not approve or say we would never do? Are we doing that because the action or person is really so offensive or potentially too harmful, or are we doing it because it makes us feel bigger or better? Typically, those kinds of comments don't make us seem wise but petty. Jesus tells us it is in our works that people will see our wisdom—or lack thereof.

Meditation: Have you ever been in a situation where, as the cliché goes, you're "damned if you do and damned if you don't"? It can be frustrating and disheartening. We don't know what to do. Nothing seems to please anyone. We may want to give up, but more often than not we soldier on and do what needs to be done, starting over every day even when it's not easy, trusting that if we do the right thing, it will be okay in the end. That is the work that spawns wisdom over contempt or judgment, the action that defies the world's tsk-tsking. We have nothing to prove. Jesus already knows our hearts.

Prayer: Jesus, we do not always have the strength to stand, as you did, in opposition to the powers of this world without bending or breaking. Give us the wisdom to do the work of the Gospel without fear, without need for approval, without accolades or reward.

Operating Instructions

Readings: Sir 48:1-4, 9-11; Matt 17:9a, 10-13

Scripture:
"Elijah will indeed come and restore all things;
　but I tell you that Elijah has already come,
　and they did not recognize him but did to him whatever
　　they pleased.
So also will the Son of Man suffer at their hands."
　(Matt 17:11-12)

Reflection: I often try to imagine what I would have been thinking or feeling had I lived in the time of Jesus and saw what everyone else saw and heard what everyone else heard. Sad to say, I'm not sure I would have been on the right team. I'm guessing I would have clung to what I knew, unable to recognize Elijah in John the Baptist or the Son of Man in Jesus. Don't get me wrong, I'd like to think I would have figured it all out in time, but that's giving myself an awful lot of credit.

So what do I do with that knowledge? What can any of us do, knowing that we didn't have to make that call and are able to judge and guess with twenty-twenty hindsight? Well, Jesus didn't leave without giving us the operating instructions. He made it pretty clear—love God and love your neighbor as yourself. If you did it to others—or withheld it from others—you did it to Jesus. We are to see God in everyone, even our enemies. We are to forgive without limit. We are to turn the other cheek, leave everything behind and follow him, be willing to die for him.

As it turns out, we do have a way of judging what we would have done two thousand years ago by what we do today. I don't know about you, but turning the other cheek and loving those who hurt me is not an easy proposition, and let's not even think about the part where we have to give up everything for God. He didn't mean that literally, right? Oh, I was afraid of that.

Meditation: Today's readings can be a challenge, so focused are they on Elijah and something that seems far removed from our lives. Try the Ignatian practice of imagining yourself in the scene. Maybe you are overhearing the conversation. Maybe you are one of Jesus' disciples. What does it feel like? Do you believe what you're hearing or are you hedging your bets, paying lip service but allowing yourself a little disbelief or doubt? Jesus asks us to be all in.

Prayer: All-knowing God, we are weak and we falter at times. Be our rock, our stronghold when doubt creeps in and begins to shake our faith. You tell us that in our weakness we are strong. Help us believe that.

THIRD WEEK OF ADVENT

Little Things Mean a Lot

Readings: Isa 61:1-2a, 10-11; 1 Thess 5:16-24; John 1:6-8, 19-28

Scripture:
   Rejoice always. Pray without ceasing. (1 Thess 5:16-17)

Reflection: Reading St. Paul's instructions in today's second reading sounds a little like Mission Impossible, not to mention a wee bit Pollyannaish. "Rejoice always. Pray without ceasing." The reality is more like this: Rejoice when something good happens. Pray when we need something. (I'm assuming I'm not the only one who falls into those bad habits.) So how do we incorporate these somewhat challenging practices into our completely challenging lives? It's actually not complicated or time-intensive. It can begin with one simple practice: gratitude.

You've probably heard spiritual gurus and self-help experts touting the power of a gratitude journal. There's a reason. It works. Writing down a few things for which we are grateful every day begins to change our perspective and our lives, and it's just a short leap from daily gratitude to ceaseless prayer. When we begin to count our blessings, we become more thankful for what we have and more aware of what others don't have. Suddenly our ordinary moments are ripe for prayer. In line at the grocery store, in the waiting room at the doctor's office, sitting in traffic—all of it is an opportunity for grace to enter in and for our lives to become a prayer. We don't have to say nonstop Our Fathers, although that is an option. What we need to do is recognize the miracles in the mundane, the divine in the everyday, and realize there is always reason to rejoice and give thanks.

Meditation: Begin a gratitude journal and try to note three things for which you are grateful. See if you can keep it up every day from now until Christmas, maybe beyond if you like the practice. The items don't have to be monumental (getting that big job); they can be seemingly insignificant but important to you (watching the first snowfall of the season). When you find yourself in a situation that starts to deplete you, find something to be grateful for. Begin to weave prayer into everyday activities—your morning commute, washing dishes, walking the dog. Start with thank you and work your way up from there.

Prayer: O God, how great thou art! Although we don't always show it, we always know it, and we are grateful for the many blessings you have bestowed on us. Give us the grace to recognize and rejoice in your unending goodness.

Crooked Lines, Crooked Lives

Readings: Jer 23:5-8; Matt 1:18-25

Scripture:
"Joseph, son of David,
do not be afraid to take Mary your wife into your home.
For it is through the Holy Spirit
that this child has been conceived in her." (Matt 1:20)

Reflection: "Do not be afraid . . ." Again and again we hear those words in Scripture, often in the face of unbelievable hardships. Joseph had every reason to be afraid, for Mary if not for himself, and yet on the word of an angel in a dream he shifts direction and does the unthinkable, at least for a faithful Jewish man of his time. Obviously, if he hadn't already been a "righteous man," as we are told earlier in today's gospel, the angel might not have been enough to convince him, so we have to assume that Joseph is made of stronger stuff than the average person, strong enough to take on a wife carrying a child that is not his own, a child who will "save his people from their sins." Did Joseph have any idea what might be ahead? Probably not, but he trusted that God would take care of him if he took the right path.

How often do we make ourselves sick with worry over things that can't begin to come close to the kind of reality Joseph faced? In situations that range from the ridiculous to the sublime, we turn over our inner peace to fear, until we feel afraid at every turn, even as we lie in bed at night. And what does all that worry get us? It rarely solves the problem and often causes new ones. Why is it so hard to trust when we can look back on our lives and see God's hand at work over and over, writing straight with our crooked lines and lives?

Meditation: Put yourself in Joseph's shoes. Do you feel betrayed? abandoned? alone? If you had a dream that told you to do the one thing that was opposed to everything you'd ever been taught, everything that made sense, would you do it, or would you chalk it up to your mind playing tricks on you? Have there been times when the Spirit was giving you clear signals—in a dream or otherwise—and you looked the other way and took what seemed like the easier route? How could you handle a similar situation differently the next time one comes along?

Prayer: Faithful St. Joseph, intercede for us today, so that we may have courage, trust, and the quiet strength that were hallmarks of your own life. Walk with us when we want to run from challenges.

December 19: Tuesday of the Third Week of Advent

Entertaining Angels

Readings: Judg 13:2-7, 24-25a; Luke 1:5-25

Scripture:
"I am Gabriel, who stand before God.
I was sent to speak to you and to announce to you this
good news." (Luke 1:19b)

Reflection: We are surrounded by angels in today's readings, a thought that put me in mind of the 1988 Wim Wenders film *Wings of Desire,* where celestial beings were ethereal in a gritty and approachable sort of way and were ever-present but unseen in the "real" world. For the audiences of both the book of Judges and the Gospel of Luke, angels were a very real and important aspect of spirituality. They were messengers from God and accepted as part and parcel of the human connection to the divine. The same cannot be said of our current culture's view of angels, where they are more often associated with whimsy, romance, and roses. How Gabriel became Cupid is beyond me, but today's readings offer us the opportunity to reflect on the possible angels in our midst, the messengers who bear God's will and word in our lives without wings and harps in both human and angelic ways.

For a long time, I avoided the angel element of spiritual life, thinking it was too childish or too faddish for serious religion, but in recent years I've become reacquainted with my guardian angel and grateful for the opportunity to give my angel—or the angels of my children and husband—an occasional (okay, maybe frequent) shout-out when the need seems especially great. I see the whole message aspect of the relationship as a two-way street, asking my angel to be my messenger back to God.

Of course, today's readings bring us angels in the most spectacular way, bearing messages of impossible things made possible through God's love and power. I think sometimes we miss our messages and messengers because we are expecting something as spectacular, but the truth is we are often entertaining angels unaware.

Meditation: The guardian angel prayer is one that we tend to learn in childhood—at least in my Irish-Italian Catholic upbringing—and so it is often associated with an immature part of faith life in our minds. Perhaps it's time to dust off that prayer and our relationship with the angel who accompanies us on our journey and take the time to rebuild what may be a lost relationship.

Prayer: Angels of God, our dear guardians, walk with us as we traverse the highs and lows of this path through our earthly life. Help us to become more aware of your unseen presence in the daily moments that test us.

December 20: Wednesday of the Third Week of Advent

Send Up a Sign

Readings: Isa 7:10-14; Luke 1:26-38

Scripture:
Is it not enough for you to weary [people],
   must you also weary my God? (Isa 7:13)

Reflection: A few years ago, the winter solstice, a full moon, and a total eclipse came together for the first time in 456 years. I remember pulling a coat on over my pajamas and standing in my driveway at 3:12 a.m. hoping to see something spectacular. I looked up and saw nothing. Thick whitish-pinkish clouds moved by, making it impossible to see the moon covered in shadow. Ever so briefly a thought crossed my mind: The moon is still there even though it's hidden from view. That was exactly how I was feeling spiritually at that point in my life as well. I desperately wanted to feel God's presence, to see God casting a shadow across my life, but I couldn't. I wanted a sign like the one described in Isaiah today: "deep as the nether world, or high as the sky!"

But those kinds of signs are few and far between. More common are the subtle signs that show up in our lives unnoticed and unannounced on a regular basis, the things that tend to fly under our radar until we're finally willing to look for the miraculous contained within the ordinary moments of our lives—the beautiful Christmas tree and strong smell of pine that took my breath away when I walked into my darkened, empty parish church, not realizing the decorating had begun; the moon hidden behind clouds on a starless winter night; the husband and children who bear my dark moods and spiritual angst amid their pre-Christmas joy, patiently waiting for me to come around and join them. Each one pours a little more light into my weary soul and reminds me that I should not wait for a sign; I should become a sign.

Meditation: Does prayer ever make you feel weary, like you never seem to get anywhere? Are you always waiting for a sign? What are you expecting? What would be enough? Is it possible the signs are already there, hidden in plain sight? Look at your life today and see if there's something hiding in the shadows, present but unnoticed.

Prayer: Merciful God, thank you for letting us come to you again and again in prayer. Give us the grace to recognize your hand at work in our lives, even when we can't see the signs. Give us the courage to say "yes" as Mary did.

Reading between the Lines

Readings: Song 2:8-14 or Zeph 3:14-18a; Luke 1:39-45

Scripture:
"Blessed are you who believed
that what was spoken to you by the Lord
would be fulfilled." (Luke 1:45)

Reflection: It's easy to get caught up in the magnificence of the whole scene in today's gospel. There is recognition that something monumental is happening not only on Elizabeth's part but even on the part of her unborn child. "And how does this happen to me, / that the mother of my Lord should come to me?"

Let's just stop right there and rewind. If we take this story at face value, we rob Mary of her humanness and, in doing so, siphon off a lot of this story's gritty power. When last we saw Mary, she was giving her fiat to the angel. Today she enters the house of Zechariah. Aren't we missing something? What happened in between? What did she tell her parents at that point? How did she get to Judah in her condition? Who went with her? What was the weather like? Was she afraid? Was she lonely? Was she confused? Was she wishing life could go back to the way things were just a short time before?

When we skip over Mary's very real struggles and jump from one mystical scene to another, we lose the woman who had the strength to say yes, who had the strength to rush to her cousin despite her own fears and worries.

Believing that what was spoken by the Lord would be fulfilled could not have been an easy proposition, at least not for the young woman who would have to see it through. When we are faced with unpleasant options and frightening prospects, it is good to look to the part of Mary absent from today's gospel—the frail humanity, the girl who says yes in faith without knowing the outcome.

Meditation: Do you ever look at someone's life from the outside and think he or she seems to have it all, or at least have it all together? When we do that, we tend to see only the public face presented to the world, and we miss the opportunity to recognize the struggle within. Try to get beyond the surface image of the people you come in contact with today. Ask a question, offer an invitation, make a connection.

Prayer: Blessed Virgin Mary, we need courage to go out and meet people where they are, to let ourselves be vulnerable before others. Intercede for us so that we might have the grace to say yes!

Finding Calcutta Close to Home

Readings: 1 Sam 1:24-28; Luke 1:46-56

Scripture:
"He has cast down the mighty from their thrones
   and has lifted up the lowly." (Luke 1:52)

Reflection: Our God is a God of surprises. Today's readings remind us of that in sometimes disturbing ways. The comfortable will be made uncomfortable, the hungry will have their fill while the full will find themselves hungry. We may shift nervously in our seats and wonder if we are among those who will be cast down or lifted up?

Most of us are blessed with warm homes and good food, clothes for every season, and ways to get from here to there. On any given day the only "concern" I might have upon waking up is whether I remembered to set the coffeemaker with Starbucks dark roast before bed. Sure, there are difficult days when disappointment and fear tear at our family, but, for the most part, I live a pretty cushy life. You wouldn't guess that from the way I whine at times.

I recently read a piece on the website Aleteia by Jeffrey Bruno, who spent some time in Calcutta. He came home to find himself having nightmares over the mere thought of being back on streets where children are "bathed in puddles that were filled with excrement." "When Saint Teresa of Calcutta arrived to serve the 'poorest of the poor,' that wasn't just a catchy little slogan . . . these, in fact, are the poorest of the poor in putrid, gut-wrenching misery," he wrote.

Few of us will be called to serve or live in that kind of a place, but all of us are called to become aware of the aching poverty that exists across the globe in Calcutta—or maybe right around the corner—and to respond, if not with hands-on ministry, then with charity and prayers. And with a sense of how blessed we really are.

Meditation: When you woke up this morning, what was your greatest worry or concern? What would it be like to wake up today and find out there is no clean water or food anywhere? If you need water, look out on the dirty streets. If you want food, dig through a trash bin. The next time a "first-world problem" threatens to derail your life, remember the poorest of the poor and try to put it in perspective.

Prayer: Jesus, open our eyes to the poverty and pain that exist around us. Soften our hearts so that we might be willing to lift others up through our prayers, words, and actions.

When Fear Gets the Best of Us

Readings: Mal 3:1-4, 23-24; Luke 1:57-66

Scripture:
Then fear came upon all their neighbors,
  and all these matters were discussed
  throughout the hill country of Judea. (Luke 1:65)

Reflection: Today we find more signs and wonders in the gospel, with Elizabeth, who had been barren, giving birth to John the Baptist, and Zechariah, who had been mute, blessing God. While there was rejoicing, we also pick up something else: an undercurrent of fear and related matters being "discussed" among the townsfolk. If those "discussions" are anything like what I've witnessed when fear and confusion run rampant, it probably sounded a lot like gossip. You can almost hear the neighbors whispering at the market: What do you make of it? Who are *they* to be given such signs, to receive God's blessings?

Fear fueled by envy and pride. We can imagine it here. We'll see more of it later on—causing Mary and Joseph to flee for their lives with their infant son, and even further down the road as John awaits execution at the hands of another Herod, who puts his own fear and pride ahead of justice and mercy.

How often do we do the same, albeit on a less brutal scope? A new person is hired at work and people scurry to gossip around watercoolers and copy machines, afraid of what change might mean. A couple splits up and friends who seem supportive on the surface whisper among themselves, Monday-morning quarterbacking about a relationship they know nothing about. A child gets into trouble at school and the parent grapevine moves into full swing with rumors and innuendos flying.

"It is so terrible to gossip!" Pope Francis has said. "At first it may seem like a nice thing, even amusing, like enjoying a piece of candy. But in the end, it fills the heart with bitterness, and even poisons us. I am convinced that if each one of us decided to avoid gossiping, we would eventually become holy!"

Meditation: Gossip is a little addictive. Focusing on someone else's flaws or troubles makes us feel better about ourselves. But, if you've ever been on the receiving end of the fallout from gossip gone awry, you know how painful it can be. Today, as you go about your business—at home, at work, in the community—be mindful of what you say, and take notice of what's fueling the need to "discuss" things.

Prayer: Merciful God, help us to be mindful of the words we say, speaking only what is true, what is necessary, what is loving.

FOURTH WEEK OF ADVENT

The Challenge of Free Will

Readings: 2 Sam 7:1-5, 8b-12, 14a, 16; Rom 16:25-27; Luke 1:26-38

Scripture:
Mary said, "Behold, I am the handmaid of the Lord.
May it be done to me according to your word." (Luke 1:38)

Reflection: The watchful waiting is almost over, and today's gospel brings us back to the moment that set these events in motion: Mary's yes to God. It's sort of like a recap, reminding us of God's decision to enter into our world as a human just like us. And yet God puts the decision into the hands of a young woman who can freely choose to say yes or no to this unthinkable request.

We are each given the same free will. Like Mary, we are presented with choices, opportunities, obstacles in this life. We can trust and move forward or refuse and freeze with fear. I think sometimes we make the mistake of thinking that saying yes to God means not having any doubt, not addressing the gnawing questions, but we wouldn't be human if we could manage that. I don't think God expects unquestioning agreement. Even Mary said, "How can this be?" God expects faith. "Do not be afraid," the angel says.

So many of our saints and holy men and women at times felt cut off from God, abandoned, without the light of faith.

A dark night of the soul. And yet they continued to say yes to God through their ministry, through their prayer life, through their willingness to be what God had called them to be even if their hearts were full of questions.

That's not an easy path, but it gives me comfort. If some of my favorite saints could have such deep—and sometimes long-lasting—questions and doubts, isn't there hope for the rest of us? We don't have to be perfect. We just have to say yes and trust in God.

Meditation: We live in a society that tells us to do our homework before we make a big decision, to read the fine print. Saying yes to God doesn't mean driving blind, but it does mean moving over to let God take the wheel. It's countercultural, this notion that we can trust what we can't see, say yes to God's will even if it doesn't make sense in a logical way. And sometimes saying yes to God means saying no to someone else. Only through prayer can we know the difference.

Prayer: Come, Holy Spirit, fill our hearts with faith, remove the clouds from our eyes, and allow us to hear and answer God's call.

SEASON OF CHRISTMAS

From Darkness to Light

Readings:
VIGIL: Isa 62:1-5; Acts 13:16-17, 22-25; Matt 1:1-25
  (or 1:18-25)
NIGHT: Isa 9:1-6; Titus 2:11-14; Luke 2:1-14
DAWN: Isa 62:11-12; Titus 3:4-7; Luke 2:15-20
DAY: Isa 52:7-10; Heb 1:1-6; John 1:1-18 (or 1:1-5, 9-14)

Scripture:
  . . . grace and truth came through Jesus Christ.
No one has ever seen God.
The only Son, God, who is at the Father's side,
  has revealed him. (John 1:17b-18)

Reflection: Winter shakes off its darkness today, reminding us that the light of our Lord, Jesus Christ, who came to us in the most unlikely way, in the most unlikely place, burns through anything our exterior world can throw at us and shines love and mercy, grace and truth into our lives. That was not a one-time gift, a past event we simply remember today. Christmas is our daily reality, born of an incarnational moment that changed all things for all time.

  God crosses the threshold of humanity to become one of us. As we look at the timeline of humankind, Christ's birth stands out as a turning point, the central axis, the thing that starts a ripple effect that is still being felt—across time, across continents.

Gifts and eggnog and tinsel hardly seem worthy of a day so monumental. As the little drummer boy sang, "I have no gift to bring . . . that's fit to give a king." The beauty is that God knows that, God embraces that. Of course we're not worthy. How could we ever be worthy, but God loves us regardless, unconditionally, eternally. Grace, truth, love, mercy revealed in human flesh. Our God is an awesome God. Joy to the world!

Meditation: As you go about exchanging gifts today and sharing holiday meals, try to keep Christ at the center of it all. When preparations make you harried, when family tensions start to rise, when gifts aren't appreciated, or when things don't go as planned, keep coming back to Bethlehem and that child in a manger, where nothing went as planned on human terms but everything went as planned on God's terms. Those are the only terms that matter.

Prayer: We praise you, Lord, for the gift of your Son born into the world today.

December 26: Saint Stephen, the First Martyr

Do You Hear What I Hear?

Readings: Acts 6:8-10; 7:54-59; Matt 10:17-22

Scripture:
But they cried out in a loud voice, covered their ears,
   and rushed upon him together. (Acts 7:57)

Reflection: We see the crowd in today's first reading acting as a crowd. They rely on mob mentality, something that has become all too familiar in our culture today. In our anger and arrogance, we often choose to move as one unthinking and cowardly collective rather than as thoughtful and courageous individuals. We get a clue as to how that begins with a few words in today's first reading that seem to serve as a warning to those of us able to judge the crowd with twenty-twenty hindsight: they "covered their ears."

Not only did they rush at Stephen as an infuriated mob, they did so even as they closed themselves off to his message and the message of God. It was as if they couldn't hear his words and attack at the same time, and so they had to make themselves deaf to the Good News. Evil had to be the louder voice or their mob may have fallen apart and with it their effort to silence what they didn't want to hear.

What does that say for us today? How often do we close ourselves off to the messages we know are meant to tell us something, meant to change our lives? Do we cover our ears—literally or figuratively—to the voice of the Spirit trying to be heard in our hearts and souls? What would happen if we unplugged our ears and tuned into the word of God at work in our lives? Would we behave differently? Would we find the courage we need to speak our truth, to speak *the* Truth even when it's difficult?

Meditation: Most of us can probably recall a time in our life when we were involved in a conversation that was going nowhere, either as the speaker or the listener. It's painful to speak the truth and have people turn on us, lie about us, and maybe even attack us. On the other hand, it's easy to try to lord it over others by shutting them out and mowing them down. We get our way, but at what cost? Today, try to be open to listening to everything, even those things that are difficult to hear.

Prayer: Saint Stephen, intercede for us today, so that we may have the courage and strength to stand up for truth in a culture that often doesn't appreciate our faith or understand our message.

December 27: Saint John, Apostle and Evangelist

Eternal Gladness

Readings: 1 John 1:1-4; John 20:1a, 2-8

Scripture:
We are writing this so that our joy may be complete.
   (1 John 1:4)

Reflection: So often we practice our faith and say our prayers, assuming that if we do it right, we will find the joy we've been seeking. Today in the First Letter of John, however, we see the reality. Our joy will not be complete until we not only incorporate our faith into our own lives but also go out and share it with others. Our faith is not meant to be kept under a bushel basket, hoarded for our own benefit, but turned out into the world.

Even if we *want* to do that, we are not always sure how to do that. We're not accustomed to the methods of some of our brothers and sisters of other faiths. We don't like to knock on doors or hand out pamphlets. In fact, we're typically not even comfortable talking about our faith even with those we know share our beliefs. We approach our faith with a very American mindset—as a private belief that should be kept out of the public square and certainly out of polite conversation.

At least, that's how it is for me. I speak about my faith on retreats and in workshops. I write about my faith in columns and in books. And yet, ask me to pray spontaneously and without advance warning, and I'm likely to pass the buck to someone else. I don't feel holy enough for that activity, and maybe that's the key. We don't wait until we're "holy enough" to share our faith or pray with others; we become holier through those very things. And when we do that, little by little we make our joy complete.

Meditation: When was the last time you spoke openly about your faith with someone outside of your immediate family? Who was it? Where was it? Were you comfortable doing it, and, from what you could tell, was the person on the receiving end comfortable hearing it? When it comes to faith-sharing, what's one thing that might help you strengthen your resolve? The next time the opportunity presents itself, step out in faith and see how it feels to evangelize. You don't have to push or convert, but rather just share in a way that fills you with joy.

Prayer: Heavenly Father, we want to follow the example of St. John, who knew that only through you could his joy be complete. Help me to follow his example and seek out true joy over transitory happiness, eternal gladness over momentary bliss.

Contradictions and Confusion

Readings: 1 John 1:5–2:2; Matt 2:13-18

Scripture:
God is light, and in him there is no darkness at all.
(1 John 1:5b)

Reflection: Our God often seems like a God of contradictions, as in today's readings, where in one breath we are told that in God there is no darkness, and in the next breath we hear of a slaughter of the darkest and most despicable kind. Then as now, when we witness tragedies of epic proportions, we wonder, "Why God?" or even "Where was God?" and, perhaps only fleetingly on some subconscious level, "If there is a God. . . ." It can be hard to reconcile the darkness we encounter in the world with the God of love we have come to know.

The slaughter of the innocents has to be one of the most "Why God?" stories in the gospels. It's hard to listen to it, and even from a place of deep and abiding faith, you can feel the confusion seep in, as if to say, surely there had to be another way. How can there be no darkness in God if this is what God has wrought?

And there is the heart of the confusion. It is not what God has wrought, but what humanity has wrought. As is so often the case, humans can be horrible and cruel and outright murderous to each other. Free will allows it, and in our weakness we humans tend to succumb to the worst temptations. God, for his part, remains constant—light in the darkness caused by human sin, whether at the hands of Herod or a modern-day version of terror and madness. Our job is to focus on the Light in the darkness and never give in to our worst fears and doubts.

Meditation: What feelings does today's gospel stir up in you? Has there been a time in your own life when you felt inconsolable in your sorrow, weeping and mourning for a loss that seemed tragic or avoidable or incomprehensible? God promises us light in the darkness, although sometimes it can seem a long time coming. Today, take some time to focus on the light and the ways God pulled you through the hardest times of your life.

Prayer: Merciful God, dry our tears and light our way as we journey through the inevitable dark moments of life. In times of overwhelming fear and sadness, allow us to feel your presence sustaining us and lifting us up.

Sorrow and Strength

Readings: 1 John 2:3-11; Luke 2:22-35

Scripture:
" . . . and you yourself a sword will pierce. . . ."
  (Luke 2:35a)

Reflection: When my first child, Noah, was born more than twenty years ago, I remember those early days after his birth like it was yesterday. There was the obvious joy and excitement over becoming a mother, but there was a strange flip side, a version of the "baby blues" that you often hear about. I would put on music and dance with Noah in our living room, crying nonstop because certain song lyrics would remind me of how delicate and uncertain life can be. I would cling to my beautiful healthy baby, smiling and crying all at once in both gratitude and fear.

I can only imagine Mary's confusion and fear during the presentation in the temple. A new mother in an already precarious situation, she is now faced with pronouncements that must have rattled her, at least on the inside. "[A]nd you yourself a sword will pierce." What a frightening statement for a new mother to hear, even one who trusts that everything is happening according to God's plan. I think we sometimes forget that Mary was a mere teenager when she bore God's son and bore these burdens of certain uncertainty.

We all know we will face sorrow and suffering, although most of us don't hear it put quite so bluntly, and yet we still manage to think we got a raw deal when it comes along. Mary's quiet and patient acceptance of her fate serves as a model for us. We do not have to like the suffering. We do not have to understand the reasons. We just have to have faith that everything is unfolding as it should.

Meditation: Imagine yourself in Mary's place today. What does it feel like to be a new parent, already worried about the safety of your family, only to hear both awesome and frightening things about the future of your son? Can you imitate Mary the next time you receive difficult news? When you start to lose hope, can you retreat to a quiet place and ground yourself in God through prayer? Try it the next time and see if it enables you to face your fears with greater peace.

Prayer: Holy Mother Mary, your unwavering yes to God gives us comfort and strength when we encounter obstacles and struggles along life's path. Intercede for us, so that we might face the unknown with faith and courage as you did.

Days of Excess

Readings: 1 John 2:12-17; Luke 2:36-40

Scripture:
Do not love the world or the things of the world . . .
the world and its enticement are passing away.
 (1 John 2:15a, 17a)

Reflection: As we prepare to close the door on another year and our annual season of excess, today's first reading hits a little too close to home. The weeks leading up to Christmas and the holiday itself are filled with too much everything—food, spending, parties, stress. Many of us end the year feeling like we have a hangover, even if we haven't had a sip to drink, and every year we vow not to repeat it the next time. We won't overbuy. We'll stick to our diet. We'll focus on the spirit of the season. But the world entices us to collect things that promise to make us happier, and, as we know all too well, those promises pass away, sooner rather than later.

Now we move into the season of undoing, of resolutions and promises that also pass away sooner rather than later. We collect diets and self-help strategies the way we do clothes and electronics, sure that one of these times we'll find the secret to success. Those kinds of plans, unless they're rooted in God, tend to end up on the figurative shelf alongside the stuff collecting dust on our actual shelf.

The transience of our resolutions stands in stark contrast to the image of Anna, the prophetess in today's gospel, who never left the temple, worshiping day and night. How foreign that seems to those of us who race through most days, often with little more than a passing nod in God's direction. We may not be able to live with such single-minded purpose, but can we find the balance between the excess John warns about and the all-consuming devotion of Anna? Can we stop swinging between the extremes of stuffed and starving and find God's middle way?

Meditation: What was your holiday season like? Did you find yourself pushing away from the tree or the table overwhelmed by the amount of stuff you consumed? Do you have plans for the New Year? Resolutions you hope to keep? Can you step back and steep those plans in prayer first, infusing them with grace?

Prayer: God of all wisdom, help us to remember that your mercy and grace do not abide by our human calendar but are available to us all the time, for all time. The one gift that never passes away.

December 31:
The Holy Family of Jesus, Mary and Joseph
(Catholic Church)

First Sunday after Christmas
(Episcopal Church)

Keep It Simple

Readings: Sir 3:2-6, 12-14 or Gen 15:1-6; 21:1-3; Col 3:12-21 or 3:12-17 or Heb 11:8, 11-12, 17-19; Luke 2:22-40 or 2:22, 39-40

Scripture:
Put on, as God's chosen ones, holy and beloved,
   heartfelt compassion, kindness, humility, gentleness,
     and patience,
   bearing with one another and forgiving one another,
   if one has a grievance against another. . . . (Col 3:12)

Reflection: Whenever I think about serving other people, I tend to think about people on the other side of the world, but often the much greater challenge is to serve the people sitting across from me at the kitchen table, or dropping socks and shoes and jackets in random places throughout the house, or leaving the dresser drawers open. Why is it such a challenge to love those who are closest to us? I know there have been plenty of times when I've jumped over kindness and gone straight to resentment over something insignificant happening around the house. That's the moment where we get to make the decision to love or not love, sow peace or sow discord.

"It is easy to love the people far away. It is not always easy to love those close to us," Mother Teresa of Calcutta said. "It is easier to give a cup of rice to relieve hunger than to relieve the loneliness and pain of someone unloved in our own home. Bring love into your home for this is where our love for each other must start."

More recently, Pope Francis gave families three key phrases to a happier, more peaceful family life: "May I?," "Thank you," and "I'm sorry." Although they are simple words, he said, they are not simple to put into practice.

The truth is that if we can start with kindness and understanding toward the most significant people in our lives—our spouse, our children, our extended families—we breed peace close to home, and only then can that peace begin to ripple outward.

Meditation: When you think of serving others, what comes to mind? Do you see your "ministry" to your family as service? The next time you fold laundry or mow the lawn or go grocery shopping, recognize that with the right perspective those daily actions are true Christian service. Peace on earth begins in our laundry room or at our dinner table, in the heart of our families.

Prayer: On this feast of the Holy Family, we pray for each other, for the safety and strength of those we love, and for all those whose family situations are difficult. We are one family. Let us treat each other with the love and respect we deserve, whether we are near or far, friends or strangers.

January 1:
Solemnity of Mary, Mother of God
(Catholic Church)

The Holy Name of Our Lord
(Episcopal Church)

Adopted into the Family of God

Readings: Num 6:22-27; Gal 4:4-7; Luke 2:16-21

Scripture:
When the fullness of time had come, God sent his Son,
    born of a woman, born under the law,
    to ransom those under the law,
    so that we might receive adoption. . . . (Gal 4:4-5)

Reflection: "Holy Mary, Mother of God. . . ." The words roll off the Catholic tongue so easily, sometimes without a second thought. For most of us, we began using those words to describe the Blessed Mother back before we could even begin to appreciate their weight, when we were toddlers or preschoolers learning our first prayers at the feet of our parents. At some point, however, as we age and begin to explore our faith more deeply, the weight of those words make us do a double take. Mother. Of. God. Not a divine mother, but a human mother—a girl, really—chosen to bear God's Son and the weight of the world, not only in her Son's lifetime but every day in things both big and small in our lives, because that's what mothers do.

Today's second reading from Galatians reminds us that God sent his Son in this way "so that we might receive adoption." What a beautiful way of putting that. Have you ever stopped to think of yourself as adopted into the family of God—chosen, protected, loved? And by extension that makes Mary our adopted mother, the mother who bore the Son of God physically and who bears each one of us spiritually, nurturing us in the womb of her heart, wrapping us in the arms of her intercession, walking with us unseen through the twists and turns of our path through life. Our mother, the mother we share with Jesus, the Mother of God.

Meditation: Think back to the days when you first learned your prayers. Was the Hail Mary among them? What did it mean to you then? What memories does it stir up? What does it mean to you now? Do you see Mary as your spiritual mother, with an interest in you and an everlasting love for you? Today, take some time to pray the Hail Mary slowly, line by line, word by word. If anything in particular jumps out at you, stay with those words for a while and come back to them throughout the day. Perhaps you can slowly say one Hail Mary every day this month, noting whether any new feelings come up or any different words or lines speak to you.

Prayer: Holy Mary, sometimes we feel like motherless children. Draw us to you at those times so that we do not lose our way.

January 2:
Saints Basil the Great and Gregory Nazianzen,
Bishops and Doctors of the Church
(Catholic Church)

Resolving to Recognize the Truth

Readings: 1 John 2:22-28; John 1:19-28

Scripture:
John answered them,
  "I baptize with water;
  but there is one among you whom you do not recognize,
  the one who is coming after me,
  whose sandal strap I am not worthy to untie."
    (John 1:26-27)

Reflection: So many of us are searching for peace, searching for the meaning of life. Often, the answer to our prayers is in plain sight, but we are either too distracted to see it or prefer to ignore it because acknowledging it might be difficult. Not much has changed since the days of John the Baptist. Then, as now, people were searching. He tells them that the person they need is already among them but they don't recognize him.

We don't always want what's good for us. Think about all those New Year's resolutions made only two days ago, some probably broken before the first day was out, others likely to be broken within weeks, only to be resolved again next year. We imagine if we fix this one thing, we'll find the peace and happiness we want, but usually what we need is very different from what we want, and often it requires us to take a long, hard look at ourselves.

John was trying to encourage the people of his own time to do just that—to look at their lives and repent, to get themselves ready for the One who was to follow him. John easily could have made claims to be something he was not, he could have basked in adulation and charted his own course toward power, but John knew who he was and he accepted that the path he needed to take would not be easy or glorious but it would be his way to peace and inner joy.

Meditation: Even if you don't make official resolutions, there are probably things you'd like to change, things you're convinced will result in the life you deserve. Look at those things more closely today. If you fix those things, will you be truly happy, will everything suddenly make sense, or is there something deeper needed here, something you don't yet recognize? Look for the unlikely or even uncomfortable path today, and sit with the possibility that what's good for you may not necessarily be on your list of resolutions.

Prayer: Today we resolve to let go and let God, and when we inevitably go back on that resolution, we ask you, Lord, to give us the courage and strength to stand up and begin again.

January 3:
Wednesday before Epiphany
(The Most Holy Name of Jesus, Catholic Church)

Choosing Connection over Isolation

Readings: 1 John 2:29–3:6; John 1:29-34

Scripture:
John the Baptist saw Jesus coming toward him and said,
   "Behold, the Lamb of God, who takes away the sin of
      the world." (John 1:29)

Reflection: Sin is a staple of our human world, and thanks to our interconnected and instantaneous communications these days, those sins seem to make headlines on a daily basis. It's easy to imagine that the real sin is not in here but out there—corrupt leaders, cheating athletes, philandering celebrities. We can convince ourselves that our sins are small potatoes by comparison and, therefore, not as dangerous. But no sin is so small that it doesn't chip away at our relationship with God, with others, and with ourselves if left unacknowledged and unforgiven. We may not make headlines because of our behavior, but sometimes the quiet sins we keep hidden are just as painful because we allow past mistakes to isolate us. We feel alone, unloved, unsalvageable.

   We're never alone and we're never past saving. The Lamb of God didn't come to save the just but to save sinners, people like us, who screw up again and again and will continue to do so until death do us part. Our humanity pretty much guarantees it. If we don't want to become trapped in self-pity and self-loathing, we need to admit our sins and accept God's forgiveness. Oftentimes we are our own worst enemies in that department, refusing God's mercy and attempting to carry our burdens alone. But that wears us out and wears us down and separates us from God. Little by little, what might start out as a fairly minor mistake drives a wedge between us and heaven, causing a rift that grows day by day.

Meditation: Have you ever had a fight with a family member or friend that left a permanent division, cutting you off from something that was once nourishing and supportive? The same can happen in our relationship with God, if we bury sins and nurse our wounds without ever seeking healing and asking for forgiveness. God's mercy is limitless, but if we hide out of fear or shame, we miss the chance to make things right and restore our connection to the divine Healer.

Prayer: Merciful Father, help us to acknowledge our sins, even those that seem insignificant, and to ask for and accept the mercy that you freely give. We do not want to be separated from your love and risk losing eternity with you.

The Ocean of Eternity

Readings: 1 John 3:7-10; John 1:35-42

Scripture:
He said to them, "Come, and you will see."
So they went and saw where he was staying,
    and they stayed with him that day. (John 1:39)

Reflection: Saint Elizabeth Ann Seton, whose feast we mark today, once said, "We must often draw the comparison between time and eternity. This is the remedy of all our troubles. How small will the present moment appear when we enter that great ocean!"

I have never been very good at seeing how small the present moment is in comparison to the bigger—eternal—picture. I get bogged down in the details of minor offenses at the office or occasional stress at home. But when I wallow in my own situation, I miss what's going on around me, which is often a lot more difficult and dire than what my day-to-day life dishes out. Many people are faced with tremendous obstacles, debilitating suffering, tragic grief, and yet they carry on, often with a far better attitude than I do on my best days. I think it comes from linking that suffering to something greater, to drawing a comparison "between time and eternity," as St. Elizabeth Ann Seton suggests.

The apostles seemed to grasp that view. When they met Jesus they immediately knew this was someone important. Andrew said straight out, "We have found the Messiah." They followed him; they stayed with him. On some level they recognized that in their lives of finite moments, Jesus represented the infinite. They left behind their small present moments (no small feat, I'm sure) in exchange for the ocean of love Jesus held out to them. He offers us the same.

Meditation: Our world can be demanding. Work hours and family obligations, volunteer committees and household chores—all of it adds up to a hard-to-manage life. We want to set our sights on eternity, but not until we get through our to-do list. God asks us to stop, to recognize the fragility of life and the reality of death. Although it sounds somber on the surface, the truth is that living with those facts at the fore will make us more joyful, more grateful, more willing to be the people we were created to be.

Prayer: Saint Elizabeth Ann Seton, as a wife, mother, widow, and founder of a religious order, you knew life from every angle. Help us to take time apart from our busy lives to focus on what matters—getting to heaven where the ocean of eternity with God awaits.

January 5:
Saint John Neumann, Bishop
(Catholic Church)

All You Need Is Love

Readings: 1 John 3:11-21; John 1:43-51

Scripture:
We know that we have passed from death to life
    because we love our brothers.
Whoever does not love remains in death. (1 John 3:14)

Reflection: We can't get to heaven unless we love others. It's a pretty straightforward message. And yet it doesn't take much more than a look at the daily headlines to see that love seems to be in short supply today.

My teen daughter, Olivia, who is working on a high school research project on human trafficking, sat at our dinner table last night and talked about the enormity of the problem of child labor in so many countries. And I thought to myself, What kind of a world do we live in where even children—maybe especially children—are not safe from abuse and violence and slavery? There has always been trouble in our world throughout history, but in today's world we are too aware, too interconnected, to let things like this happen. We are better than this, aren't we? But we often feel powerless to stop it.

Somehow in our hyper-connected world, our global village, we have lost sight of each other, we have forgotten that we are part of one family. How do we recover that knowledge? How do we live that truth?

By taking baby steps. If we look at the big picture, it's completely normal to feel overwhelmed and paralyzed by the enormity of what's in front of us. When we take that view, it's easy to do nothing because we don't know where to begin. But if we break it into smaller pieces—a community organization that needs donations, a parish-sponsored event to help the unborn or refugees, even our very own dinner table each night—we begin to see that we can make a difference and we do have a purpose. What's your purpose?

Meditation: Perhaps if we can do some soul-searching and discover the ever-elusive answer to that question, we can begin to plant the seeds of real peace. But it will take more than platitudes; this requires practice, action. Today's first reading reminds us that we need to love "not in word or speech / but in deed and truth." What might that look like in your life? How could that kind of love transform the world?

Prayer: God of love, sometimes our vision is clouded by the us-against-them message preached by secular society. Help us to see clearly the moral imperative to stand up for the helpless, speak for the voiceless, and love all.

January 6:
Saturday, Christmas Weekday

The Epiphany
(Episcopal Church)

The Uncomfortable Truth

Readings: 1 John 5:5-13; Mark 1:7-11 or Luke 3:23, 31-34, 36, 38

Scripture:
The Spirit is the one who testifies,
   and the Spirit is truth. (1 John 5:6b)

Reflection: I just sent my husband, Dennis, off on a weekend retreat at the Trappist Abbey of the Genesee in western New York this morning. Tucked into his backpack is a note I hope he'll find later telling him that, while I hope he'll enjoy the rest and peace that a silent retreat offers, I know at the same time that it will be a challenge. Prayerful solitude and silence is not an easy proposition, which is why most of us avoid it at all costs. That is where the Spirit testifies and speaks truth to us, and, quite frankly, God's truth is not usually a cakewalk. It's much easier to say we are busy and go about spinning from one task to another rather than shut everything down and simply listen.

Today, as we near the end of the Christmas season, the readings seem to urge us on one last time to get right with God, to fully understand what unfolded in that stable in

Bethlehem two thousand years ago and what continues to unfold in our own lives every single day. God sent his son, became one of us, trod this earth, stood in the Jordan awaiting baptism, broke bread with his apostles, died on a cross, rose from the dead. Do we believe what the Spirit testifies to us? Sometimes I think that if my faith ran deeper than it does, if it rose to the level of biblical proportions, everything would change in an instant. How could it not? If my mind could wrap itself around the incarnation in a profound way, I would never be the same. And that's a scary prospect. So I fill the silence with noise and try to avoid the only thing that can save me.

Meditation: Where do you go when you want to listen to the Spirit—out in nature, your parish church, your garden or kitchen? When was the last time you put away all the "stuff" that normally fills your day and just listened? Can you do that today? Right now? Can you do it every day, if only for five minutes? Begin today and watch what happens when you allow the Spirit to testify in your life.

Prayer: Holy Spirit, today we invite you to enter into this quiet space and speak to our hearts. Help us to hear the truth, even if it's not easy or comfortable.

EPIPHANY AND BAPTISM
OF THE LORD

January 7:
The Epiphany of the Lord
(Catholic Church)

Signs from the Sky

Readings: Isa 60:1-6; Eph 3:2-3a, 5-6; Matt 2:1-12

Scripture:
"We saw his star at its rising
  and have come to do him homage." (Matt 2:2b)

Reflection: I am one of those people fascinated by the moon and stars. I'll run outside in stocking feet to catch a glimpse of a full moon rising or a sliver of a crescent hanging by a thread in the night sky. But, when I think about it, I'm sort of fickle. I don't do the day-by-day watching of the stars the way my husband does as he walks our rescue dog every night. On the rare occasions I join him, he can tell me the exact position of the Big Dipper and which way it's tracking, or he'll point to a bright light—sometimes Venus, sometimes Mars—steady and strong amid the twinkling lights.

For the magi, the stars were not simply a light show or entertainment. They were their way of life and their guiding lights—literally. They knew on that night in Bethlehem that something had shifted, that a light emerged that could not, should not be ignored, and so they followed, without question, despite tremendous obstacles and dangers.

I wonder, if we paid similarly close attention to our surroundings and the subtle shifts in our environment, might we notice when God was speaking to us in an obvious way? Would we be drawn closer to God with such force that an encounter would be unavoidable? So often we ask God to show us a sign, but when the sign appears we are too distracted or too afraid to follow it.

Meditation: Go outside tonight and look up at the stars. What do you see, and, more importantly, what do you feel? Perhaps it's cloudy and you can't see much, or you live in a city where the electric lights drown out the natural ones. Perhaps it's cold and uncomfortable. Perhaps it's perfectly clear and you catch a glimpse of the Milky Way or at least a critical mass of stars. Imagine seeing something in the sky tonight that would propel you to leave home, with your belongings on your back, in search of the One who would change the world for all time. Sit or stand under the night sky in silent prayer for a few minutes.

Prayer: God of the Universe, shine your light into our lives and guide us on right paths, so that we, like the magi, may never lose sight of the path to Jesus amid the struggles of our lives.

January 8:
The Baptism of the Lord
(Catholic Church)

Just Push Pause

Readings: Isa 42:1-4, 6-7 or Isa 55:1-11; Acts 10:34-38 or
1 John 5:1-9; Mark 1:7-11

Scripture:
Peter proceeded to speak to those gathered . . . saying:
  "In truth, I see that God shows no partiality.
Rather, in every nation whoever fears him and acts
    uprightly
  is acceptable to him." (Acts 10:34-35)

Reflection: Our starting point in faith, in life is from a place
of unconditional love and acceptance by our God, who
"shows no partiality." Not a bad way to begin. So why do
we forget that? Why do we always seem to think we are too
broken, too difficult, too scarred to be loved by God for who
we are? Somehow we imagine God will love us only after
we're fixed, forgetting that the only way out is through.

As we close out the Christmas season and head back into
Ordinary Time, we are called to carry with us what we began
these past few weeks, but it's not so easy or simple. The
special seasons call us to shift our focus onto God, but everyday life can get in the way of that. It overwhelms us and

tells us to do too many things at once, to fill up the pauses with things that seem more productive. We know better now.

The pauses are where life with God begins. Like the rests in a symphony that keep the music from becoming a mishmash of sound, the pauses shape our days and our journey, if we're willing to be countercultural.

Dorothy Day once said, "The greatest challenge of the day is: how to bring about a revolution of the heart, a revolution which has to start with each one of us?" Are you willing to start a revolution, even if you're the only one participating? That's how transformation begins, one by one, heart by heart. There's nothing ordinary about that.

Meditation: As we move away from the glow of the holiday season back toward life in the "real" world, without the tinsel and ribbons, it can be easy to backslide to our pre-Advent attitudes, rushing without pausing, working without resting, talking without listening. As you go through your days, try to check in with God at least twice a day—once upon waking and once before sleeping. It doesn't have to take long, it doesn't have to be elaborate, it doesn't even have to have words. Just breathe in and out and let the Spirit do the rest.

Prayer: All-loving God, we thank you and praise you for the many gifts and blessings you have given us, for your mercy and love, for your unshakable presence in our lives. God, you are great, all the time.

References

December 5: Tuesday of the First Week of Advent
Teresa of Calcutta, Nobel Peace Prize lecture, Nobelprize.org, December 11, 1979, https://www.nobelprize.org/nobel_prizes/peace/laureates/1979/teresa-lecture.html.

December 9: Saturday of the First Week of Advent
Francis, Chrism Mass homily, Saint Peter's Basilica, March 28, 2013, http://w2.vatican.va/content/francesco/en/homilies/2013/documents/papa-francesco_20130328_messa-crismale.html.

December 22: Friday of the Third Week of Advent
Jeffrey Bruno, "I'm Back from Calcutta and Still Having Nightmares," Aleteia, September 15, 2016, http://aleteia.org/2016/09/15/im-back-from-calcutta-and-still-having-nightmares/.

December 23: Saturday of the Third Week of Advent
Francis, Sunday Angelus message, Saint Peter's Square, February 16, 2014, https://w2.vatican.va/content/francesco/en/angelus/2014/documents/papa-francesco_angelus_20140216.html.

December 31: The Holy Family of Jesus, Mary and Joseph
Teresa of Calcutta, *Life in the Spirit: Reflections, Meditations, Prayers*, ed. Kathryn Spink (New York: HarperCollins, 1983), 38–39.

Francis, Address of Pope Francis to Engaged Couples Preparing for Marriage, Saint Peter's Square, February 14, 2014, https://w2.vatican.va/content/francesco/en/speeches/2014/february/documents/papa-francesco_20140214_incontro-fidanzati.html.

January 4: Saint Elizabeth Ann Seton, Religious

Elizabeth Ann Seton, *Elizabeth Bayley Seton: Collected Writings, Volume II*, ed. Regina Bechtle and Judith Metz (Hyde Park, NY: New City Press, 2002), 156–57.

January 8: The Baptism of the Lord

Dorothy Day, *Loaves and Fishes: The Inspiring Story of the Catholic Worker Movement* (Maryknoll, NY: Orbis, 1997).